Photography by:
Günter Ziesler, Leslie Groff

LION FAMILY
Jane Goodall

A MADISON MINI BOOK

Published by Madison Marketing Limited.
Madison Marketing Limited holds the exclusive
license to this edition.
Copyright © 1991 by Neugebauer Rights & Licenses AG., Zurich.
Text copyright © 1991 by Jane Goodall.
All rights reserved.
ISBN 1-55066-014-4

Printed in Canada

Printed on recycled paper

LION
FAMILY
Jane Goodall
ANIMAL SERIES

*P*hotographs selected by
Michael Neugebauer

Madison Marketing Limited

I'll never forget the evening three male lions invaded our camp. Our African cook was preparing supper when suddenly he looked up – and there was a lion's head stuck through the tiny kitchen tent! He threw pots and pans at the lion until it went away. Another lion investigated the cook's sleeping tent. The tent was zipped shut, so he tore a hole in the side with his powerful claws. Finally all three lions came prowling around the tent where my husband and I were waiting for our supper. And then they wandered off into the African night.

They were just curious. Until a few months before they had lived with their family group or pride. But when they were almost grown, the adult males of their pride had pushed them out into the world to find their own food and their own females.

I knew their pride well. We were camped in their hunting grounds on the Serengeti plains in Tanzania. There were three lionesses, two big males and six half-grown cubs. The two males, Leo and Simba, were brothers. Once they had roamed on their own, after being driven out of the pride where they were born. And now they had a pride of their own.

Tawnie was about nine years old. The other two lionesses, Amber and Jade, were younger. The six cubs were all that remained of the babies that had been born the year before. There had been 13 to start with, but the African plains can be cruel. Many cubs die because there's not enough to eat, or they're killed by other hunters like hyenas or leopards.

Jade, Amber and Tawnie usually hunted together. First they looked for a small herd of wildebeests, zebras or antelopes. They placed themselves around the edges of the herd, always making sure that their powerful cat smell was not blowing toward the animals. Tawnie was the most experienced and often selected the prey.

She would creep forward inch by inch, getting as close as she could before charging. It's an amazing sight to see a lioness stalking. She uses every tiny shrub or tuft of grass to break up her distinctive lion shape. If one of the prey looks toward her she freezes until the animal relaxes and begins to feed or move again. And then she suddenly charges, a streak of golden fur and powerful muscles. Tawnie would chase the prey toward one of the younger lionesses who made the kill. I always hated to watch them killing other animals. But they had to eat, and usually they strangled their prey quickly. Then the lionesses fed, eating as much as they could before Leo and Simba charged up and took over the carcass.

Male lions usually leave the hunting to the females. It's harder for males to hide because of their great manes. And since they're so big and strong, they can easily keep the females from feeding until they've eaten their fill. But when Amber, Jade and Tawnie killed a very large animal, Leo and Simba would let them share. The youngsters always had to wait until the adults had finished.

The lions of a pride are very friendly with each other. After feeding they lie close together, dozing in the shade of a tree. When they greet they rub up against each other and purr.

On the Serengeti there is a long dry season when no rain falls and the plains become dry, brown and dusty. The lions find it hard to get food. Yet Amber got fatter and I knew she was going to have babies. She had three. For four weeks they stayed hidden away behind some big rocks, blind and helpless like newborn kittens. When they came out and began to play in the sunshine they tumbled and tripped over every stick and rock.

Soon they got stronger and more agile, and played just like kittens. They chased insects, pounced on leaves that blew in the wind, and jumped onto each other and rolled over and over.

Amber left her cubs on their own in the den while she went hunting with the pride. When she came back and called to them with low mewing sounds they tumbled out with little cries of pleasure. She licked them, rubbed her huge head against their tiny bodies, then rolled over on her back so that they could suckle. Afterwards they curled up and went to sleep.

When the cubs were eight weeks old Amber led them to join the rest of the pride. The six young lions were the first to investigate the new babies. The cubs spent a lot of time playing, wrestling and chasing, pouncing and swatting. Almost everything they did in their games served as practice for the stalking and hunting skills that would help them survive as adults.

When Amber's cubs were a little older, she'd fetch them after a kill had been made so they could learn to eat meat instead of drinking milk. She'd growl and snarl at them when they tried to suckle, and bat at them with her paws. These cubs were lucky, though – Jade would let them nurse from her. The females of a pride always share responsibilities in this way. Sometimes Leo would let the little ones play with his tail. When he began to get irritated he waved his tail, just like a cat. And then the cubs pounced more and more wildly, and he got more irritated and waved his tail faster – and in the end he usually snarled and hit them away with one of his huge paws.

The year-old cubs were now learning how to hunt, and followed the lionesses when they went hunting. At first they were more of a nuisance than a help, but gradually they got better. This was especially important for the young males who would soon be driven away by Leo and Simba and forced to fend for themselves.

Leo and Simba are young and strong, and well able to defend their family from roaming rival males. At night the air is often shaken by their great roars. Amber, Jade and Tawnie join the chorus. The roars die away to low coughing grunts. From the far distance the voices of the other lions reply, rising above the sounds of the African night – the calling of hyenas, the lowing of the wildebeests, and the high-pitched barking of the zebras. Magnificent, beautiful and free. No wonder the lion is known as King of the Beasts.

*J*ANE GOODALL has shared her important discoveries and her love of animals with millions of people around the world through books, films and lectures. She has founded ongoing research and educational institutes on two continents, and is one of the world's most acclaimed naturalists.

The Jane Goodall Institute for Wildlife
Research, Education and Conservation
P.O. Box 41720, Tucson, AZ 85717 U.S.A.

The Jane Goodall Institute — Canada
P.O. Box 3125, Station "C"
Ottawa, Ontario K1Y 4J4 Canada

The Jane Goodall Institute — U.K.
15 Clarendon Park
Lymington, Hants SO41 8AX United Kingdom